Meg's book

Illustrated by Nina O'Connell

Meg's eggs   page 2

The log   page 6

The big seed   page 11

PRINCETHORPE INFANT SCHOOL
WEOLEY CASTLE
BIRMINGHAM

Nelson

Meg's eggs

I have one egg.
Look at my egg,
said Meg.

I have two eggs.
Look at my eggs,
said Meg.

I have three eggs.
Look at my eggs,
said Meg.

Come and see my eggs.
Come and look.

The log

One chick got on the log.

Two chicks got on the log.

Three chicks got on the log.

Fat Pig got on the log.
No, no, no,
said the chicks.

The big seed

Here is a seed, said Meg.

It is very big.

I will plant it.

So she did.

I will get it some water,
said Meg.
So she did.

Look at it now, said Meg.

I will get it some more water.

So she did.

The seed grew and grew.

It grew as big as the chicks.

It grew as big as Meg.

The seed looks like the sun,
said Meg.

It is a sunflower.

We can eat all the seeds, said Meg.

And they did.